The Missions of California

Mission
San Juan Bautista

Allison Stark Draper

The Rosen Publishing Group's
PowerKids Press™
New York

For my parents and my brother.

Published in 2000 by The Rosen Publishing Group, Inc.
29 East 21st Street, New York, NY 10010

First Edition

Photo and Illustration Credits: pp.1, 21, 29, 31, 39A, 45, 47, 50, 51 © Cristina Taccone; p.4 © Shirley Drive; pp. 5, 9, 10, 30, 37A, 39B, 43, 44 © North Wind Picture Archive; pp. 6, 11, 22, 28 © CORBIS/ Bettmann; pp. 7, 13, 27, 33, 37B by Tim Hall; pp. 8, 35 © SuperStock; pp. 12, 14, 15, 20, 23, 41 © Michael K. Ward; pp. 17, 26, 36 © Department of Special Collections, University of Southern California Libraries; p. 24 © The Bancroft Library; p. 38 © Archive Photos; p. 42 © Shirley Jordan; pp. 48, 49A, 49B, 49C Courtesy of Glenn Farris; p. 49D by Mrs. Anna Semenova; pp. 52, 57 © Christine Innamorato.

Book Design: Danielle Primiceri

Editorial Consultant Coordinator: Karen Fontanetta, M.A., Curator, Mission San Miguel Arcángel
Editorial Consultant: Ruben G. Mendoza, Ph.D, Associate Professor, California State University, Monterey Bay;
        Institute Director, Institute of Archaeology
Historical Photo Consultants: Thomas L. Davis, M.Div., M.A. and Michael Ward, M.A.

Draper, Allison Stark
    Mission San Juan Bautista / by Allison Stark Draper
        p. cm.—(The missions of California)
    Includes bibliographical references and index.
    ISBN 0-8239-5501-X
    Summary: Discusses the mission at San Juan Bautista from its founding in 1797 to the present day, including the reasons for Spanish colonization in California and the effects of colonization on the Mutsun (a tribe of Costanoan) Indians.
    1. San Juan Bautista (Mission: San Juan Bautista, Calif.)—History Juvenile literature. 2. Spanish mission buildings—California—San Juan Bautista Region—History Juvenile literature. 3. Franciscans—California— San Juan Bautista Region—History Juvenile literature. 4. Costanoan Indians—Missions—California—San Juan Bautista Region—History Juvenile literature. 5. California—History—To 1846 Juvenile literature. [1. San Juan Bautista (Mission: San Juan Bautista, Calif.)—History. 2. Missions—California. 3. Costanoan Indians—Missions. 4. Indians of North America—Missions—California. 5. California—History—To 1846.]
    I. Title. II. Series.
    F869.S3947D73 1999
    979.4'75—dc21   99-24063
                                                        CIP

Manufactured in the United States of America

Contents

The Spanish Colonize the Americas

Mission San Juan Bautista

At the foot of the Gavilán Mountains in California is the small, beautiful city of San Juan Bautista. Walking into San Juan Bautista is like stepping back in time. White houses line the pale, dusty streets. Bronze church bells ring in the blue sky. Roses bloom along the sidewalks from May until September. People say that San Juan Bautista feels more like the olden days than anywhere else in California.

The city of San Juan Bautista got its name from a mission that was built there more than 200 years ago. Mission San Juan Bautista was founded on June 24, 1797. It was the 15th of 21 missions built by the Spanish along the coast of California from San Diego to Sonoma.

The Franciscans

In the late 1700s, the Spanish government sent a group of Franciscan friars, or *frays*, to establish the mission settlements. The Franciscans belonged to an order of Catholics founded in 1209 by Saint Francis of Assisi. The Franciscans believed in living simply, studying the Bible, and teaching others about their religion. They established the missions to teach the American Indians in California about Christianity and to bring Spanish culture to the Americas.

▲
Saint Francis of Assisi.

◀ *Mission San Juan Bautista today.*

The Spanish View of the American Indians

At that time, most Europeans believed that the Christian religion and the culture of Europe were superior to all other religions and cultures. They thought that anyone who was not a Christian would not go to heaven when he or she died. They also thought that anyone who lived differently from the way the Europeans did was uncivilized. The Spanish believed that God wanted them to convert the American Indians to Christianity. They also believed that they would be helping the American Indians if they taught the Indians to dress and act like the Spanish. They did not realize that by teaching the American Indians to be like the Spanish, they would destroy many Indian cultures.

Spanish Interest in the Missions

The Spanish government was interested in California because it wanted to expand the borders of Spain, own more land, and rule more people. Spain did not have enough people who wanted to leave their homes to colonize the Americas. If Spain wanted to claim land there, it would have

to find another way to populate it with Spanish citizens. The government decided to send Franciscan friars to teach American Indians about the Catholic religion and about Spanish dress, trades, and customs. If the Franciscans converted the Indians to Christianity and taught them to act like Spanish citizens, the Spanish

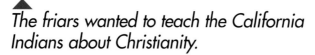

The friars wanted to teach the California Indians about Christianity.

government would be able to claim California as part of Spain without having to go to war with the Indians. Once the American Indians had been made into Spanish citizens, they could also be made to pay taxes to the Spanish government.

The Spanish government did not think about what the American Indians wanted. When the Franciscan friars arrived in California in the late 1700s, California Indians had been living there for thousands of years. They had their own religions and cultural traditions and were no more interested in becoming Christians than the missionaries were in becoming Indians.

Why Some California Indians Converted

The Franciscan friars came to California with many more resources than the California Indians had. The Spanish had guns and soldiers and the support of the Spanish empire. They had beads and other gifts that they gave to the California Indians. They had farming skills and tools that allowed them to have a steady supply of food all year round. Over time, the Franciscans converted many California Indians and brought them to the missions. There the Indians practiced Christianity and worked in the fields of what swiftly became Spanish California. The traditions, rituals, and religious beliefs of many of these Indians were neglected and forgotten. Much of the history of the California Indians is now lost forever.

▲
Many California Indians converted to Christianity and worked in the mission fields.

The Spanish Missionaries

Cortés and the Aztecs

Shortly after Christopher Columbus sailed to the Americas in 1492, a Spanish explorer named Hernán Cortés sailed to the land that today

Hernán Cortés.

is Mexico. At that time, Mexico was ruled by people called the Aztecs. The Aztec empire was vast, ancient, and very rich. Cortés wanted to conquer the Aztecs and claim their gold and their land for Spain. The Aztecs were fierce and powerful fighters. Their empire was made up of many tribes that they had conquered and enslaved. Cortés convinced the leaders of these tribes to band together into an army and fight for their freedom against the Aztecs. He led this army against the Aztecs and defeated them through a combination of military skill and luck. Cortés's military strength came from the fact that he and his army had horses and guns, while the Aztecs had neither. Cortés's luck was a result of the diseases, like smallpox and typhus, that Cortés and his soldiers had accidentally carried with them from Europe. The Europeans had some immunity to these diseases, but the Aztecs, who had never encountered them before, did not. As a result, many Aztec warriors died of illness before they even reached the battlefield.

New Spain

The Spanish became the rulers of the Aztecs' land and their people.

Cortés and his army defeated the Aztecs in 1521. ▶

The Spanish named the country New Spain and began to settle there. Over the next 200 years, Mexico City grew into a thriving Spanish colony. By the 1700s, it was filled with schools, hospitals, and churches. The Spanish owned the land and ran the government. They ruled the people and treated them as their subjects. The Spanish set up missions in New Spain and later in the peninsula of Baja (meaning lower) California. They brought Indians to the missions by offering them food and gifts. They taught the Indians farming and Spanish trades. They taught them the Spanish language and converted them to Christianity.

Alta California

To the north of New Spain was California, which the Spanish called Alta (meaning upper) California. The Spanish wanted to claim the land in Alta California as well. In 1769, acting on the orders of King Carlos III of Spain, the ruler of New Spain, called a viceroy, sent an expedition north into Alta California. The expedition included soldiers, mule drivers, Indians

who had converted to Christianity, and Franciscan friars, including one named Fray Junípero Serra. When Fray Serra joined the expedition to Alta California, he had been in New Spain for almost 20 years, teaching Spanish, preaching, and converting people to Christianity. Because of his hard work in New Spain and Baja California, Fray Serra was chosen to lead the new missions in Alta California. He

▲
Fray Serra, the first president of the Alta California missions.

was named as the first president of the Alta California mission system and remained so until his death in 1784. Fray Serra founded nine of the missions in Alta California. He is remembered as the legendary pioneer of El Camino Real, the road that connects the 21 Alta California missions.

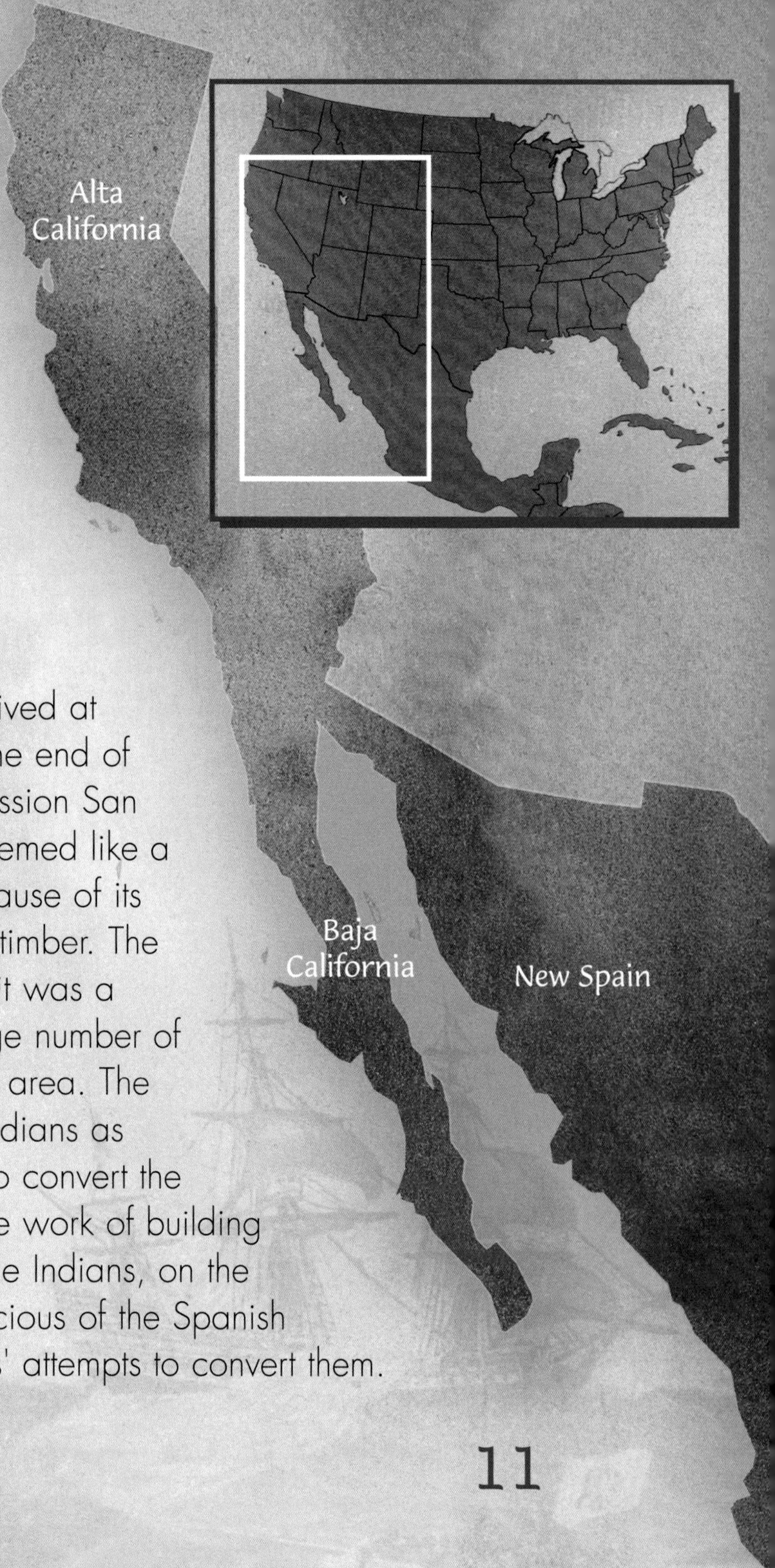

Fray Serra and his men arrived at the site of the first mission at the end of June 1769. They named it Mission San Diego de Alcalá. The area seemed like a good place for a mission because of its nearby supplies of water and timber. The missionaries also thought that it was a good spot because of the large number of California Indians living in the area. The missionaries always viewed Indians as Christians-to-be. They hoped to convert the Indians and get them to do the work of building and farming at the mission. The Indians, on the other hand, were at first suspicious of the Spanish invaders and resisted the friars' attempts to convert them.

Alta California

Baja California

New Spain

The Mutsun Indians

The Mutsuns

Most of the California Indians who lived in the area where Mission San Juan Bautista would eventually be built were Mutsun Indians. Within 40 or 50 miles, there were several Mutsun tribes. Each of these tribes spoke slightly different versions, or dialects, of one language. They shared basic methods of hunting, fishing, cooking, and building.

The Mutsuns lived in beehive-shaped huts that they wove from flexible branches, tule reeds, and willow leaves. These houses were perfectly suited to the mild weather in central California. It was warm during most of the year, and it rarely snowed. In the summer, it was so warm that the Mutsun women dressed in short aprons and the men often wore nothing at all. In the winter, both men and women wore cloaks lined with soft rabbit fur.

Hunting and Gathering

Mutsun men fished and hunted for food. They hunted squirrels, rabbits, otters, and other small animals. They also hunted larger game, like elk and deer. They carved sharp spear points and arrowheads from rocks and obsidian. The women gathered plants, acorns, berries, and seeds to eat. Acorns were a very important source of nutrition for the Mutsuns, and the women ground them into flour to make porridge and breads. Acorns have some poison in them, so the

▲ *Mutsun men hunted and fished.*

◀ *Mutsun women gathered and prepared food, and cared for the children.*

women rinsed the flour with hot water 10 times to make it safe to eat. Then they let the flour dry and stored it for later use.

The Mutsun women made baskets from grasses and strips of wood. They used the baskets to store food, carry supplies, trap fish, and cook. The Mutsun women wove their cooking baskets so tightly that they could hold water. They boiled the water for cooking by dropping in rocks that they heated in the fire.

Games

The Mutsuns loved to play games and to gamble. They played a sport that was like field hockey, and they gambled with marked wooden sticks. They also loved music and dancing. They carved flutes and whistles out of the bones of geese and deer. They made rattles by carving hollow balls into the ends of small sticks and filling them with gravel.

▲
The Mutsuns played games of chance with marked wooden sticks.

▲
The friars taught the California Indians about Christianity and the Spanish way of life.

Beliefs

The Mutsuns had many beliefs and rituals that were specific to their culture. For instance, although the Mutsuns hunted and killed animals for food the way the Europeans did, they had a respect for life that was sometimes hard for the Europeans to understand. It was traditional for a Mutsun hunter or fisher to respond to a catch with a feeling of sorrow for the death of a fellow creature. In the same situation, a European hunter might be pleased rather than sad. When the Spanish began to convert the Mutsuns to Christianity, they not only changed the religious ideas of the Mutsuns, but also their way of looking at the world. As a result, many parts of Mutsun culture, not just the games and rituals, but the different ways in which the Mutsuns understood the world, were forgotten or lost.

Founding Mission San Juan Bautista

Choosing a Site

Mission San Juan Bautista was built to fill a gap between two existing missions along El Camino Real. The Franciscans and the Spanish government wanted the missions to make travel along the coast of Alta California easy. The Spanish did not feel safe traveling at night through Indian lands. Mission San Juan Bautista closed a stretch between Mission San Carlos Borromeo del Río Carmelo and Mission Santa Clara de Asís that left travelers vulnerable to night attacks on the open road.

Teaching Christianity to the California Indians was not the only purpose of the missions. They also offered shelter and safety to new Spanish settlers who the government hoped would come to live in Alta California. The government of New Spain knew that the sooner Alta California was populated with Spanish farmers and ranchers, the sooner it would really belong to Spain. Therefore, the government was determined to make El Camino Real as safe and welcoming a road as possible.

A soldier named Hermenegildo Sal led the expedition to find a site for Mission San Juan Bautista. He was accompanied by Fray Antonio Dantí, who kept a record of the trip. The party set out on November 15, 1795. On the journey, Fray Dantí wrote that they saw three Indian men and seven Indian women as well as an abandoned Indian village of 27 homes. The small number of California Indians in the area worried the friars. They wanted to find a large Indian population that they could convert and use to work on the mission. If there were not many California Indians, there would be no one to convert, and farming and building at the mission wouldn't be successful.

The expedition party reached the banks of the San Benito River on

Mission San Juan Bautista was built to close the distance between two other missions. ▶

November 16, 1795. The river was dry, and they followed it to its source, hoping to find water. On the 17th, they examined the plain below the river and found two pools that could be used as wells. They found timber in the form of willow, poplar, alder, and redwood trees, tule for roofing, and limestone that could be used for building foundations. The soil was excellent for farming and gardening. Sal and Dantí decided that the area looked like a good place for a mission. They set up a large cross to mark the spot. The cross symbolized the Christian religion and showed that the Spanish were claiming this area for themselves.

When the new president of the California missions, Fermin Francisco de Lasuén, received Dantí's report, he thought the site sounded ideal. It was well placed to close the distance between Mission San Carlos Borromeo del Río Carmelo and Mission Santa Clara de Asís. Even

San Francisco de Solano
San Rafael Arcángel
San Francisco de Asís
San José
Santa Clara de Asís
Santa Cruz
San Juan Bautista
San Carlos Borromeo del Río Carmelo
Nuestra Señora de la Soledad
San Antonio de Padua
San Miguel Arcángel
San Luis Obispo de Tolosa
La Purísima Concepción
Santa Inés
Santa Bárbara
San Buenaventura
San Fernando Rey de España
San Gabriel Arcángel
San Juan Capistrano
San Luis Rey de Francia
San Diego de Alcalá

though Sal and Dantí had only seen a few California Indians, Fray Lasuén knew that there were many tribes in the area. Near the site and west toward the coast, there were many Mutsun villages, and in the valley to the south, there were Yokut tribes.

Fray Lasuén recommended the building of the new mission near the site of the cross. He sent a man named Corporal Ballesteros and five other soldiers from the Monterey presidio, or military fort, to the site. The soldiers built temporary buildings so that the friars would have someplace to live and a church to worship in when they arrived. By June 17, 1797, Corporal Ballesteros and his men had built a church, a house for the friars, a guardhouse for the soldiers who would watch over the mission, and a granary. The site was ready for the arrival of the friars.

The Founding Ceremony

On June 24, 1797, Mission San Juan Bautista became the 15th mission in Alta California. Fray Lasuén came to perform the founding ceremony himself. He blessed the site and performed a Mass. He named Fray Joseph Manuel de Martiarena and Fray Pedro Adriano Martinez as the first friars at the mission.

The size of the cross raised at Mission San Juan Bautista impressed the Mutsuns and Yokuts. A legend arose among these tribes that the cross was more powerful than the local Indian altars. Because of the legend, many Mutsuns and Yokuts believed it was wise to stand in the shadow of the cross and become a Christian. Perhaps even more convincing than the cross were the gifts that the Spanish gave the Indians. The Mutsuns and Yokuts who came to the founding ceremony were given food, as well as beads and other trinkets, and encouraged to stay and work.

19

Building Mission San Juan Bautista

Adobe Buildings

After the founding ceremony, work on the mission began almost immediately. The buildings that the Monterey soldiers had made were quickly constructed out of wooden planks and covered with mud roofs. These wooden buildings could be damaged easily by stormy weather and earthquakes. They could also catch fire from the open flames used for cooking and for heat. The friars wanted their mission to be made of more lasting materials. Like most of the missions in Alta California, Mission San Juan Bautista would be made out of adobe bricks coated with white plaster. Adobe buildings are strong, and they are cool in the summer and warm in the winter. Fray Martiarena and Fray Martinez worked quickly to begin the adobe buildings at the mission.

Adobe is a mixture of soil, water, and cut straw. The friars taught the Indians who came to the mission how to make the adobe and mix it with their feet. The Mutsun and Yokut Indians trampled the cut straw into the clay, molded the mixture into bricks, and dried the bricks in the sun.

▲

An adobe wall.

The Building Progresses

The Indians at Mission San Juan Bautista worked quickly. By December 31, 1797, seven buildings had gone up. An adobe chapel, 42 feet by 17 feet, was built and roofed with mud and tules. A home for the missionaries was built of

◀ *The friars sometimes worked with the California Indians to build the missions.*

21

the same materials. In addition, there was a granary, a house for unmarried women called a *monjerío*, a kitchen, a guardhouse, and four houses for the soldiers at the mission.

The work of ranching began right away as well. Livestock were donated to Mission San Juan Bautista by other missions. The mission had 115 cattle, 140 sheep, 4 pigs, and 6 horses. Most of the farming would not begin until the next year.

Neophytes

As the building and ranching progressed, Fray Martiarena and Fray

▲

Indians being baptized.

Martinez were also teaching the Mutsuns and Yokuts about the Christian religion and how to speak Spanish. When the friars felt that the Indians had learned enough about Christianity, they baptized them. Baptism is the ceremony that takes place when someone is accepted into the Christian religion. After they were baptized, the Indians were called neophytes, which meant that they were new to the faith. The neophytes had to live at the mission and obey the friars. They could not practice their old religion or live as they had before they were baptized. If they disobeyed the friars, they could be punished and even beaten.

Early Problems at the Mission

In 1798, California Indians from the mountains east of Mission San Juan Bautista surrounded the mission at night and prepared to attack. Soldiers with guns convinced the Indians to give up and leave the mission before the fighting could begin. Later, many of the neophytes at the mission ran away to join the attackers. Soldiers were sent out to capture the neophytes and bring them back. A chief was killed in the fighting, another was wounded, and two California Indians from the mountains were brought back to the mission by force. Fifty of the neophytes who had run away were captured, brought back to the mission, and beaten.

The tribes from the east struck back at the mission by killing two neophytes and burning a house and a wheat field. The soldiers returned to the villages and captured 18 California Indians, including two chiefs.

Even though Mission San Juan Bautista was having troubles, building continued. A large adobe granary, 146 feet by 22 feet, was

The neophytes were sometimes punished by being whipped.

built. That year also marked the first planting and harvest at the mission. Crops of wheat, barley, corn, beans, and peas were all grown in large quantities.

Earthquakes

The mission continued to face problems. What Fray Dantí and Hermenegildo Sal did not know when they recommended the site for Mission San Juan Bautista was that the land they chose lay on a fault. A fault is a split inside the earth that causes earthquakes. Mission San Juan Bautista had been built directly on the San Andreas fault.

In October 1800, there were several weeks of terrible earthquakes. On October 31, Sal reported that shocks had occurred from October 11 to October 30, sometimes as many as six in a single day. All of the mission buildings were damaged. It was so frightening that the friars and the neophytes slept outside for a whole month.

An Enclosed Community

At the end of 1800, Mission San Juan Bautista had made great progress. Over 500 neophytes had converted and come to live at the mission. They had harvested 2,700 bushels of grain that year, and the number of livestock was steadily growing. The mission was on its way to being a self-sustaining community that could grow, raise, or make almost everything it needed.

The friars planned to build the mission much like the other missions, in the shape of an open square, or quadrangle. The

Mission San Juan Bautista.

mission quadrangle would include: the church; the *convento*, which was the friars' living quarters; the *monjerío*; kitchens; dining rooms; workshops; storage rooms; and granaries. Within the mission quadrangle was a courtyard. Outside of the walls of the quadrangle were: the *ranchería*, or the neophyte village; orchards; fields; corrals for the animals; and the cemetery. *Ranchos* were established a few miles away from the mission where there was more land for grazing the livestock. Each *rancho* usually had a house for the neophytes, a chapel, and a corral.

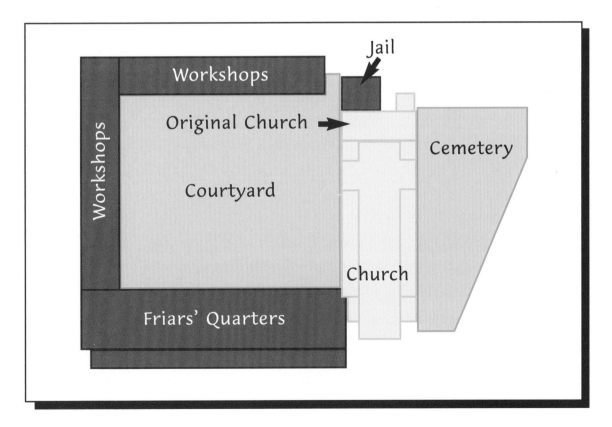

Life at Mission San Juan Bautista

Work

Daily life at Mission San Juan Bautista followed a strict schedule. Bells were rung to call the neophytes to wake, pray, eat, and work. The

▲
The bells were rung to keep the mission community on schedule.

neophytes at Mission San Juan Bautista grew food for everyone at the mission. They made their own clothes, blankets, dishes, and shoes. Everybody at the mission worked. People planted, cooked, sewed, herded cattle, and raised children. Even the children worked, gathering fruit in the orchard and watching the animals.

The men and married women worked outside the mission walls in the *ranchería*, in the gardens, in the orchards, and on the farms. They raised squash, melons, beans, and corn. In the orchards, they tended the figs, grapes, pears, and olive trees that the friars had imported from Spain.

The unmarried girls and women lived inside the mission quadrangle in the *monjerío*. They worked in the kitchens, the kitchen garden, or the sewing room. They made bread, cooked stew, and ground olives into oil. They grew fruit and vegetables. Women carded wool and cotton, and sewed shirts and dresses. They knitted socks and blankets. They wove storage and cooking baskets out of grass and willow twigs. They swept and mopped the mission buildings and the mission church. They washed their clothes and the friars' clothes in the washing area called the *lavandería*.

The friars directed the neophytes' work at the mission. ▶

Olive Oil

One of the most important jobs at Mission San Juan Bautista was the women's job of making olive oil. Children gathered olives from the orchard. Then the women poured them into a stone olive mill. They tied a mule to a wooden beam that was attached to the mill and led the mule in a circle. This turned a giant stone at the bottom of the mill and crushed the olives. The women then pressed the oil from the crushed olives and stored it in large clay jars.

Olive trees were very important to the success of Mission San Juan Bautista.

Olive oil was important because the friars were able to trade the oil for things that the people at the mission could not produce themselves. In the early days, the neophytes grew or made everything that

Altar decorations were acquired through trade.

was needed at Mission San Juan Bautista. As time went on, and more and more people settled in Alta California, the friars were able to trade

The church pulpit.

for things the neophytes at the mission could not make. Some of the goods they received in these trades were necessities, like iron kettles and pottery, and some were luxuries, like silk, coffee, honey, and decorations for the mission church.

Men and Women

The friars believed that unmarried women should live apart from men. Unmarried women and girls over the age of nine had to stay inside the *monjerío*. When a girl was 15 or 16, she often became tired of living inside the *monjerío*. She wanted to meet a young man and marry him. After she had married, she could move into a house in the *ranchería* with her husband and raise a family.

The Mission Grows

Tile Roofs

In 1801, work on the buildings in the mission quadrangle continued. A new project was begun as well. Until this time, the roofs of the mission buildings had been covered with mud and thatch. These materials caught fire easily. Beginning in 1801, the neophytes at Mission San Juan Bautista began to make roof tiles. The neophytes made the rounded red roof tiles out of clay. They created the shape by molding the wet clay over wooden logs.

Roof tiles.

Rancho La Brea

In 1803, the governor of California demanded that the friars remove their livestock from one of the mission's *ranchos*, Rancho La Brea. The governor had sold it to a Spanish man named Mariano Castro. Fray Martiarena and Fray Doningo Iturrate, who had come to replace Fray Martinez, refused to give up the *rancho*. They wrote a letter to the viceroy of New Spain. Fray Martiarena and Fray Iturrate said that the *rancho* belonged to the neophytes at the mission and that the land could not be given to anyone else. The viceroy agreed with them, and Rancho La Brea was saved.

A New Church

By this time, the neophyte population had grown so much that Fray Martiarena and Fray Iturrate decided that they needed to build a

◀ *Mission San Juan Bautista had beautiful plants and trees in its gardens.*

bigger church. In June 1803, the cornerstone of the new church was laid in the ground. In 1804, Fray Martiarena retired to New Spain, and a man named Fray Andrés Dulanto came to take his place. The stone foundation of the new church was laid, more buildings were added to the quadrangle, and a wall was built and topped with tiles.

In 1805, the neophytes began to build adobe homes in the *ranchería*. By 1806, many of these homes were completed, the mission quadrangle was finished, and the adobe walls of the new church were being built. Ranching and farming were successful enough to produce food and clothing for everyone at the mission.

Runaways and Conversions

In 1805, it was recorded that 200 neophytes ran away from Mission San Juan Bautista. There were still hundreds of neophytes left. The neophytes did most of the work that made the mission productive. For this reason, the missionaries were always interested in increasing the neophyte population.

In 1806, Mission San Juan Bautista sent an expedition out to Yokut villages, hoping to bring more neophytes to the mission. The expedition left on September 21, led by a soldier named Gabriel Moraga, who had come from the presidio in San Francisco. The men traveled for 43 days, reaching Mission San Fernando on November 2, 1806. Along the way, they managed to convert 141 Indians who were very old or dying. It was often easier for the friars to convert people who were sick or about to die. The friars believed that only Christians who had been baptized would go to heaven. When they told dying people about all the terrible things that they believed would happen to them, the dying people often became frightened and agreed to be baptized. Since all of the 141 Yokuts who were baptized were sick or old, none of them left their villages to come to live at the mission.

▲

California Indians who were sick were often more willing to be baptized than those who were healthy.

The Mexican Revolution

New Spain Becomes Mexico

On September 16, 1810, the people of New Spain revolted against Spain and began a war for independence. They said that the new name of their independent nation was Mexico. Because Mexico was in the middle of a war, it did not have much money. Officials there could not send money or supplies to the Alta California missions as they had before. They also couldn't afford to pay or send supplies to the soldiers in Alta California.

Life at the Mission Changes

That year, there were 702 neophytes at Mission San Juan Bautista. Many were dying of European diseases to which the American Indians had no immunity. In addition to the hardships of illness, life at the mission began to change because of the war in Mexico. The first sign was the lack of gifts, such as scarves, games, toys, sweets, holy pictures, and musical instruments that the neophytes normally received from the friars. The Spanish government had always given the friars at each mission $400 each year. The friars had often spent this money on supplies and gifts to keep the neophytes happy.

The neophytes suddenly had to work harder to produce more food, tallow, and wool, and to raise more livestock. Since the government was no longer supporting the soldiers, and the soldiers would not work to support themselves, the missions were forced to supply them with food and clothing. Even though the neophytes at Mission San Juan Bautista now worked even longer and harder than before, they still were not paid for their labor.

Mexico began its war for independence in 1810. The war lasted until 1821, when Mexico ▶ *became an independent nation.*

Map of North America

Circle • M. Mackenzie in 1789 • Mackenzie R. • R. Coppermine • The Sea seen by M. Hearne in 1771 • Buffalo I.

Eric's Fir. • Whale • Bedford • E. in of Zaal • Sandersons Tour • Walsingham • Baals R. • C. Farewell • Land Brig.

Repulse Bay • Fort in 1631 • Broken Land • Raleigh • Cumberland Str. • Troubles Str. • Resolution I. • STRAIT • Straits enter'd by Capt. Brown • C. Chidley • Hillsborough I. • Davis Inlet • Byrons Bay • Sandwich B.

Theyc Creek Point L. • Cogead L. • Chesterfield Inlet • Marble I. • Nottingham • Southampton • Mansel • Musquito Harb. • Nth. Sleepers • Nain • Moravian Settlement • Oglincoloke • Drucktokoe • Red Bay • White B. • C. Charles • Belisle

Horn Mt. • Mehye L. • Doobaunt L. • Neville Bay • St. Bobeys • Button's B. • NEW NORTH WALES • HUDSONS BAY • Portland Pt. • Bakers Dozen • Hopewell H. • Richmond Bay • Atchi Kounipi • Ashwanippi • Macating • NEW FOUND LAND

Slave • Peace R. • Athapescow L. • Churchill • Knights Hill • Ft. Bay • Solitary I. • Committe • Lookout • East Main • Ounabuskol • Red Bay • C. Charles • Anticosti • Georges B. • St. Lawrence • C. Ray • C. Breton • Louisbn.

STONEY MOUNTAINS • La le Cross • Cumberland H. • Hudsons H. • Cedar L. • NEW • Nascus R. • SOUTH WALES • Henrietta Maria • Vincers • Albany f. • Mistassins • Canso • C. Sable

NEW HANOVER • NEW GEORGIA • Buckingham Ho. • Manchester Ho. • Winnipeg L. • Cat L. • Gloucester Hou. • Moose Ft. • Brunswick • St. Peters L. • Abbitibbe L. • Tenis camina L. • Quebec • NOVA SCOTIA • Halifax

P. Vancouver • L. Missouri R. • Assenaboye R. • F. Dauphin L. • Osnaburg Ho. • Saul L. • L. of the Woods • L. Eel • L. Sturgeon • White Bear L. • Bear L. • Falls of St. Anthony • CANADA • Mishipicoton • Nipissing • R. Tawas • Montreal • L. of the Woods

R. St. Peter • Lake Superior • Huron • L. Ontario • Oswego • NEW VERMONT • Rhode I. • Long I. • Portsmouth • Boston • C. Cod

Teguayo • Missouri R. • Moin R. • Mississippi River • L. Erie • Albany • York • Philadelphia • NEW JERSEY • ATLA

St. Francisco • Puerto de Monterrey • P. Estero • S. Pedro • Leyxao • Sta. Fe • NEW • New Madrid • St. Francis • UNITED • Ohio • Lexington • KENTUCKEY • Washington • VIRGINIA • Williamsburg • Baltimore • C. Charles • Chesapeak B. • Albemarle S.

Quiquimoo • S. Felipe • LOUISIANA • STATES • TENNESSEE • N. CAROLINA • Newbury • C. Hattcras • C. Lookout

Yumas • MEXICO • S. Marie • R. Colorado • Arkansas R. • Black R. • Red R. • Akansas • Upper Creek • Augusta • S. CAROLINA • Wilmington • Fear R. • Pedaw R.

Velicata • S. Paul • Rio Bravo • Cenis • New Orleans • W. FLORIDA • GEORGIA • Darien • Marys R. • Charlestown • Savanna

Llerres • CALIFORNIA • NAVARRE • F. Janoi • Texas • St. Antonia • Lorello • Augustin • Cannareral • OCE

B. Magdalena • St. Juan Baptista • Conception • GULF • Blat • Apalachy B. • Spirito Santo • Charlotte • Chatham • OF • E. FLORIDA • Bahama I. • Abacco • BAHAMA • Eluthera

C. St. Lucas • Marias I. • Conception • Rio Bravo • MEXICO • Martyrs • Havana • Guanahani • Little I. • Long ISLES

C. Corientes • Mechoacan • Mexico • Compostella • B. Blanche • Nassau • CUBA • Cocos • Turks I. • Handkerchie

Zaatula • P. de S. Tuspan • Ulloa • Delgado • P. Piedra • Mindi • Cosumel I. • Antonio • C. Cruz • S. Yago • St. Mark • ST. DOMINGO • Porto Rico

Acapulco • GUATEMALA • Guaxaca • MEXICO • BAY OF HONDURAS • Savanna le Mar • Jamaica • Kingston • S. Domingo

NEW • Salvador • Cape • Gracios a Dios • CARIBBEAN SEA • LEEWARD ISL.

▲

The finished church and part of the quadrangle.

The Church Is Completed

Work in the mission fields, ranches, and workshops was exhausting, but the neophytes still found the energy to continue building Mission San Juan Bautista's church. The church was finished and then blessed on June 23, 1812.

Mission churches were very different from mission buildings used for working and living. The Franciscans felt that a building devoted to God should be more beautiful than other buildings. Franciscans took an oath of poverty, so they did not have much furniture or many decorations in their rooms. The church, on the other hand, was for God, and the friars felt that it should be decorated for him. Therefore, the mission churches contained beautiful oil paintings, gold crosses, and chandeliers, while buildings for working and sleeping contained only simple wooden furniture.

▲
A friar's chair at Mission San Juan Bautista.

The church at Mission San Juan Bautista is the largest and most unusual of the mission churches. Most of the others are long and narrow, and have only one aisle down the middle of the church. Mission San Juan Bautista's church has three aisles that together hold a thousand people.

Fray Tapis

In 1812, Mission San Juan Bautista was honored by the decision of the mission president, Estévan Tapis, to retire there. Fray Tapis wanted to create a real Catholic choir at Mission San Juan Bautista. He picked a group of young neophyte boys with good singing voices and taught them to sing like a European choir. He invented a special way of color coding the music so that the boys could read it and follow along as Fray Tapis played the pipe organ.

▲
Some friars, like Fray Tapis, taught music.

One day, while Fray Tapis was playing and the boys were singing, a group of Yokut Indians raided the mission. Fray Tapis kept playing as loudly as he could. The boys started to sing at the tops of their voices. The Yokuts were so surprised to hear boys from their own tribe singing along to the strange sound of the pipe organ that they stopped to listen and ended the raid.

When Fray Tapis arrived at Mission San Juan Bautista in 1812, he ran it with the help of Fray Felipe de la Cuesta. Fray Cuesta was very interested in the culture of the neophytes at the mission. He helped to preserve the Mutsun language by writing it down.

Another Attack

In 1815 and 1816, bands of Yokut Indians attacked Mission San Juan Bautista several times, stealing horses and murdering some of the neophytes. In 1818, 32 Yokut Indian neophytes ran away from the mission. Later that same year, a group of Yokuts nearly stole 40 mares and mules from Mission San Juan Bautista, but the noise of the attack woke a group of neophytes. They chased the thieves and recaptured the animals.

▲
The mission was attacked several times.

The Mission Grows

Despite its problems, the mission continued to grow. In 1815, a dormitory was built for single men and widowers at the mission. Seven adobe homes with tile roofs were built in the *ranchería*. The inside of the church was decorated as well. The church's altar was designed by Fray Tapis, built by the neophytes, and painted by a Boston sailor named Thomas Doak. Doak jumped ship in 1816. He did not want to be dragged back to sea or thrown in jail, so he asked to stay at Mission San Juan Bautista. The mission did not have enough money to pay an artist who asked for about 75 cents a day for his work. Doak agreed to paint

Stairs painted by Thomas Doak.

the mural in exchange for food and a place to sleep. Doak was probably the first American to settle in Alta California.

Many neophytes joined the mission.

Thirty-two neophytes ran away in 1818. Although the mission was doing well, not everyone was happy there. The strict schedule, lack of freedom, and fear of European disease were all reasons that neophytes sometimes fled from the mission.

In 1821, the people of Mexico won the war against Spain. Alta California now belonged to Mexico. Mexican officials were not sure what they wanted to do with the missions in Alta California. In 1821, there were 1,248 neophytes living at Mission San Juan Bautista. This was the largest number of neophytes that would ever be at the mission.

Tragedy

In 1825, Fray Tapis died and the friars and neophytes at Mission San Juan Bautista mourned. That same year, heavy rains collapsed two corrals, which had to be rebuilt. By 1830, Fray Cuesta was so ill that he had to be carried on a stretcher to fulfill his duties. Fray Juan Moreno was sent to the mission to assist him.

Secularization

In 1834, the Mexican government secularized the missions, which means they took them away from the church. The mission *rancherías* and farmlands were no longer run by the Franciscans. The Mexican government emancipated the neophytes. They said that the neophytes were free to leave the missions and make their own way in the world. Mexican officials were sent to run the mission lands that were not sold and to rule over the Indians who did not leave the missions.

On December 19, 1834, a Mexican official named Antonio Buelna went to Mission San Juan Bautista to tell the neophytes that they were free. Many of the neophytes had been born at Mission San Juan Bautista and knew nothing of life outside of the mission. Some traveled to the growing cities of California to look for work. Some returned to their tribes. Others found themselves without food, work, or protection for the first time in their lives.

By 1835, there were only 63 neophytes left at Mission San Juan Bautista. The Mexican government tried to provide for these Indians by giving them some of the mission lands and livestock. Half of the mission lands were made into a group farm called a common. This arrangement did not work very well. After years of taking orders from the friars, the Indians found it difficult to run the mission without a leader and without soldiers to enforce the rules. They also had to deal with ranchers who wanted to take the mission lands for themselves. Constant Yokut raids interfered with any attempts to keep farming. By 1840, even the orchards of Mission San Juan Bautista were nearly ruined. All that remained of the *ranchería* was a little settlement of 50 people huddled around the San Juan Bautista church.

▲
Some California Indians returned to their tribes after the missions were secularized.

The End of the Missions

Governor Micheltorena

The last hero of the Alta California mission system was Governor Manuel Micheltorena. In the 1840s, he briefly returned the secularized missions to the Franciscans. Micheltorena had many enemies among Mexican landowners who wanted the mission lands for themselves. Several of these landowners met at Mission San Juan Bautista and decided to drive Micheltorena from the country.

Micheltorena organized a small army to defend himself but was unable to defeat the landowners. Finally, on February 22, 1845, abandoned even by his own Mexican soldiers, he resigned in disgust and left Alta California for good.

The Mission Is Sold

Governor Micheltorena was replaced in February 1845, by Governor Pio Pico. Governor Pico saw the rich farmland of the failing mission system as a chance to make some money. On September 4, 1845, Governor Pico took an inventory of the goods and crops at Mission San Juan Bautista. He estimated the total value of the mission to be $7,860. Then he sold it in a secret auction. The friars who had established the mission were not allowed to operate it anymore. The California Indians who had lived in the area before the Spanish arrived lost most of their land forever.

▲
Governor Pio Pico.

◀ *Mission San Juan Bautista.*

Americans Come to Alta California

At this time, many Americans were moving west to Alta California to set up shops and businesses. Some were outlaws who escaped prison in the United States by running away to Alta California. Others married into powerful Mexican ranching families. Some bought land and started ranches of their own. The Americans who lived in Alta California usually became Mexican citizens, learned Spanish, took Spanish last names, and became Catholics. There were other Americans who wanted to make Alta California an English-speaking part of the United States.

▲
John C. Fremont.

One of the people who believed that Alta California should become an American state was Lieutenant Colonel John C. Fremont. When the Mexican War broke out in 1846 between the United States and Mexico, Fremont went to Mission San Juan Bautista. He stayed at the mission and gathered horses and weapons to fight the Mexicans.

Fremont raised an army of 428 men. After several battles, Fremont met with a Mexican named Andrés Pico. They signed a peace agreement called the Treaty of Cahuenga, which forced Mexico to give California to the United States and ended the war. On July 7, the United States Marines landed in California and raised the American flag. California became a part of the United States and was named the 31st state in 1850.

Effects on the Mutsuns and Yokuts

After the Mutsun and Yokut neophytes left Mission San Juan Bautista, most of them were unable to return to their old way of life. California had changed a great deal as a result of Spanish, Mexican, and finally American colonization. As years passed, some of the Mutsuns married settlers and had children who were only part Mutsun.

The last full-blooded Mutsun Indian was born in May 1855. Her name was Ascension Solórzano de Cervantes. During her life, she worked to preserve the language and history of the Mutsun people by writing it down. The Mutsuns had an oral, or spoken, tradition, which means that Mutsun children learned Mutsun history and legends by listening to the stories of their parents and grandparents. Cervantes tried to make sure that as the Mutsun community shrank, Mutsun history would be saved in books.

Cervantes lived to be 75 years old. She died on January 29, 1930, and is buried in the old Indian cemetery beside the church at Mission San Juan Bautista.

Ascension Solórzano de Cervantes's grave.

Mission San Juan Bautista Today

The Mission Is Preserved

Mission San Juan Bautista has fared better than most of the California missions over the years. The church at Mission San Juan Bautista is the largest of the mission churches, and it still looks almost exactly the way it did nearly 200 years ago when the Mutsun and Yokut Indians began building it in 1803. Inside the church, three parallel aisles run from the altar to the two towering, carved wooden entrance doors. Pressed into the floor just beyond the doors are the paw prints of an animal who ran across the still-wet floor tiles just before they dried.

The mission did suffer a violent earthquake in April 1906, but in 1907, the town held a festival, called a *fiesta,* to raise money to fix the church. The highlight of the *fiesta* was the replacement of the huge cross that Hermenegildo Sal erected in 1795. The cross had stood two miles from Mission San Juan Bautista for over half a century until it was chopped down in the 1850s by a local farmer who had used it as a gate post.

An Archaeological Find

Even though the main buildings of the mission are unchanged, there is always more to learn about Mission San Juan Bautista. In 1991, an archaeologist named Glenn Farris explored the soil of the old *rancheria.* He discovered two buildings buried under years of dirt and dust.

The buildings were probably the homes of neophyte families. The buildings are both over 200 feet long. The smaller building has 11 rooms. The larger one has 22 rooms. Inside the buildings, Farris found artifacts of daily life. He found pestles for pounding acorns into flour.

Many school groups visit Mission San Juan Bautista today. ▶

He found iron scissors and a brass thimble for sewing clothes. He found knives from New Spain. He found Indian jewelry made of shells and glass trade beads.

Farris also found a 10-inch ramrod for packing gunpowder into a pistol that may have belonged to a Spanish soldier. Archaeology is like detective work. Who owned that pistol? Who wore those glass beads? Why were these things left behind in the buried buildings?

◀ *Phil Hines, a state archaeologist.*

▲
Glenn Farris, a state archaeologist.

▲
Judy Husted, a volunteer excavator.

Clay figures found at the site. ▶

◀ *Iron knife blades and kettle parts found at the site.*

This drawing shows what the neophyte housing at Mission San Juan Bautista probably looked like in the 1820s.

Iron nails found at the site.

49

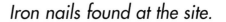

Visiting Mission San Juan Bautista

Today, the mission church at San Juan Bautista belongs to the Catholic Church. Catholic priests hold services there just as the friars did in the old mission days. The church is open to the public. Tourists can walk along the three aisles, peer into the baptismal font, and admire Thomas Doak's painting. They can examine the artifacts in the museum and imagine the stories of the people who owned and used them. They can walk into the courtyard of Mission San Juan Bautista and look up at the unchanged range of the Gavilán Mountains. Sometimes, for a moment or two, the smell of the dust and the sound of the water splashing in the fountain will sweep them back to the old mission days of early California.

Some of the exhibits at Mission San Juan Bautista.

Mission San Juan Bautista is an active church today.

Make Your Own
Mission San Juan Bautista

To make your own model of the San Juan Bautista mission, you will need:

cardboard	fake flowers/trees	miniature bells
beige paint	sand	scissors
white paint	masking tape	ruler
toothpicks	foamcore board	X-Acto knife (Ask
cardboard	glue	for an adult's help.)

Directions

Step 1: Use a foamcore board that is 15" by 16" for your base. Paint this beige. Let dry.

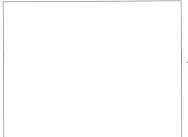

15"

16"

Adult supervision is suggested

Step 2: For the facade (the front) of the church, cut a piece of cardboard with dimensions as shown below.

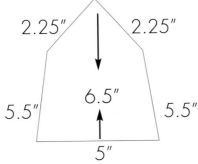

Step 3: Cut out doors and a window. Cut two pieces of cardboard 5.5" by 1". Tape these to the sides of the facade as shown below.

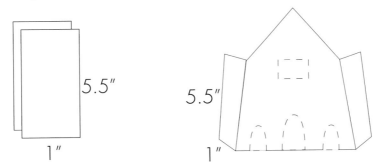

Step 4: For the sides of the church, cut two pieces of cardboard to measure 6" by 10". For the front and back, cut two pieces of cardboard to measure 6" by 9.5".

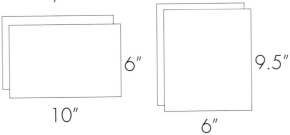

53

Step 5: Tape these pieces together to form a box shape. Glue to your base.

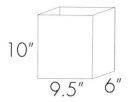

10"

9.5" 6"

Step 6: Glue toothpicks horizontally and vertically to the inside of the facade window. Then tape the small side walls of the facade to the front of the box.

Step 7: To make the four building extensions on each corner of the church, cut 12 pieces of cardboard to measure 6" by 2".

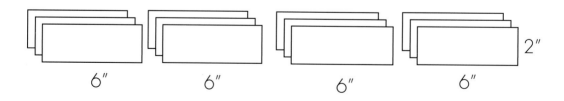

6"   6"   6"   6"

2"

Step 8: Tape three of the pieces cut in Step 7 together to form a box shape with a missing side. Tape this to the left back corner of the church, the open end facing the church wall.

Step 9: Repeat this process three more times. Tape each three-sided structure to a corner of the church. Glue to the base.

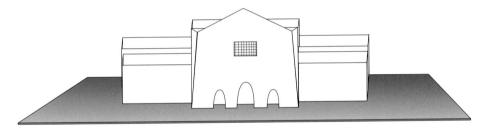

Step 10: Cut out four pieces of cardboard to measure 3" by 2" for the bell tower. Cut two large, arched windows out of one piece. This is where two bells will hang.

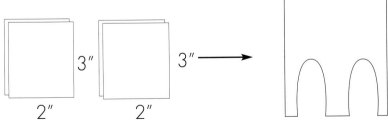

Step 11: Tape these four pieces together to form a box. Tape to the right front corner of the church.

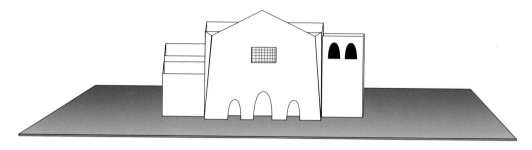

Step 12: Cut a piece of cardboard in an arch 3" by 2". Cut an arched window out of this and tape to the top of the bell tower.

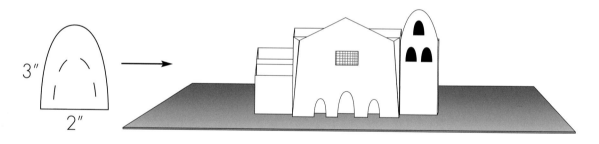

3"

2"

Step 13: Paint whole mission with white paint mixed with sand. Decorate with greenery.

Step 14: For the roof, cut corrugated cardboard as shown below and glue to the top of the church. Stick toothpicks through the bells and glue behind the windows.

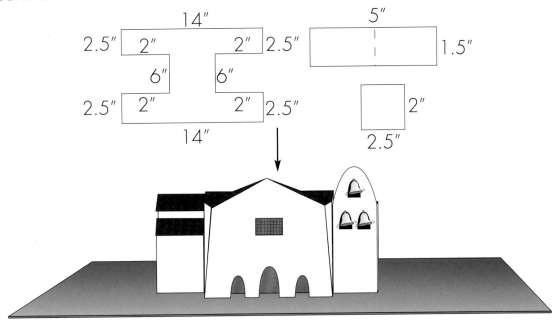

*Use the above mission as a reference for building your mission.

Important Dates in Mission History

1492	Christopher Columbus reaches the West Indies
1542	Cabrillo's expedition to California
1602	Sebastián Vizcaíno sails to California
1713	Fray Junípero Serra is born
1769	Founding of San Diego de Alcalá
1770	Founding of San Carlos Borromeo del Río Carmelo
1771	Founding of San Antonio de Padua and San Gabriel Arcángel
1772	Founding of San Luis Obispo de Tolosa
1775–76	Founding of San Juan Capistrano
1776	Founding of San Francisco de Asís
1776	Declaration of Independence is signed
1777	Founding of Santa Clara de Asís
1782	Founding of San Buenaventura
1784	Fray Serra dies
1786	Founding of Santa Bárbara Virgen y Mártir
1787	Founding of La Purísima Concepción de Maria Santísima
1791	Founding of Santa Cruz and Nuestra Señora de la Soledad
1797	**Founding of** San José, **San Juan Bautista**, San Miguel Arcángel, and San Fernando Rey de España
1798	Founding of San Luis Rey de Francia
1804	Founding of Santa Inés Virgen y Mártir
1817	Founding of San Rafael Arcángel
1823	Founding of San Francisco de Solano
1848	Gold found in northern California
1850	California becomes the 31st state

Glossary

adobe (uh-DOH-bee) Sun-dried bricks made of straw, mud, and sometimes manure.

aisles (IYLS) Straight passageways.

archaeologist (ar-kee-AH-luh-jist) A scientist who studies the bones, objects, buildings, and other remains of people from the past.

architecture (AR-kih-tek-chur) The art of designing buildings.

artifacts (AR-tih-fakts) Objects that were made by humans.

baptism (BAP-tih-zum) A ceremony performed when someone is accepted into, or accepts, the Christian faith.

Catholicism (kuh-THAH-lih-sih-zum) The faith or practice of Catholic Christianity, which includes following the spiritual leadership of priests headed by the Pope.

Christianity (kris-chee-A-nih-tee) A religion based on the teachings of Jesus Christ and the Bible, practiced by Eastern, Roman Catholic, and Protestant groups.

convert (kun-VIRT) To change from belief in one religion to belief in another religion.

empire (EM-pyr) A large area, usually including many different peoples, ruled by one government or leader.

Franciscan (fran-SIS-kin) A communal Roman Catholic order of friars, or "brothers," who follow the teachings and example of Saint Francis of Assisi, who did much work as a missionary.

friar (FRY-ur) A brother in a communal religious order. A friar can also be a priest.

granary (GRAY-nuh-ree) A building where grain is stored.

livestock (LYV-stahk) Farm animals kept for use or profit.

Glossary

Mass (MAS) A Christian religious ceremony.

neophyte (NEE-uh-fyt) The term for someone who is newly converted to Christianity.

quarters (KWOR-turz) Rooms where someone lives.

ramrod (RAM-rod) A metal stick used for packing gunpowder into a gun.

ranching (RAN-ching) Raising cattle, horses, or sheep on a farm.

rituals (RIH-choo-wulz) The special ceremonies of a religion or culture.

secularization (seh-kyuh-luh-rih-ZAY-shun) When control of the mission lands was taken from the church and given to the government.

thatch (THACH) A covering for a house made up of reeds and grass bundled together.

viceroy (VYS-roy) A governor who rules and acts as the representative of the king.

villages (VIH-lih-jiz) Original communities where American Indians lived before the arrival of the Spanish.

Pronunciation Guide

convento (kahn-VEN-toh)

El Camino Real (EL kah-MEE-noh RAY-al)

fiestas (fee-EHS-tahs)

fray (FRAY)

lavenderí a (lah-vahn-dehr-EE-ah)

monjerí o (mohn-HAYR-ee-oh)

rancherí as (RAHN-cher-EE-as)

ranchos (RAHN-chohs)

Resources

To learn more about the Mission San Juan Bautista and the missions of California, check out these books and Web sites:

Books:

Bleeker, Sonia. *The Mission Indians of California.* New York, NY: William Morrow and Company, 1956.

Oh California. Boston, MA: Houghton Mifflin Co., 1991.

Web Sites:

General information:
http://www.hollinet.com/~sjb/aboutsjb.html

History:
http://www.hollinet.com/~sjb/history.html

Archaeology:
http://www.indiana.edu/~maritime/caparks/crm/sjb/sjb.html

General history and mission information:
http://coyote.rain.org/~serra/serra.htm
http://tqd.advanced.org/3615/tour3.html

Index